G&T?
GRIN & TONIC

Funny, true stories to make you smile!

No 1 BEST SELLER!
(probably)

joey parkin

Alcohol-free fun in a book!

Boring but important copyright bit:

No part of this book is allowed to be reproduced or copied, in any form including photocopying, without begging me, the author and creator for permission. (I love Jaffa cakes and mint Matchmakers).

I've made a darn good effort to ensure this book contains accurate information (plus some totally made up stuff) but I am not liable for any loss or damage suffered by readers as a result of any information contained in it. (How did I know you were going to hurl it at your lazy husband in a moment of madness? Haven't you heard of anger management? Well then).

Illustrated by little old me.

SYNOPSIS

This wonderful little book wraps it's arms around you (without making you feel uncomfortable), gives you a big warm hug and makes you laugh again.

It explores the fragility and irony of human nature with humour and honesty to give you a rare glimpse into the curiously creative mind of contemporary artist and designer Joey Parkin - a self deprecating social misfit with an eccentric sense of humour and a penchant for the written word.

A must for everyone who requires a little light hearted relief from the frustrations of modern life. A tasty tonic, to be absorbed daily for maximum effect. It contains lots of funny and often poignant snippets, observations, poems and sketches to give you "the feel-good factor". This will last far longer than any other stimulant (without the nasty side effects). It is however, highly addictive.

Acknowledgements

This book is dedicated to my children Jodie and Jake Parkin who inspire me every day and are my greatest achievements. My Keveroony who calms my madness and (worryingly) shares my sense of humour.

My bezzy mate Angela who is just plain freaky (in a good way) and encourages me to be myself. "Skipper" my first love (a unique Border collie) who was my best friend and guardian and "H" my cat who was my soul mate.

My parents for making me, my sisters Mandy and Jayne, for making allowances for me and Morrissey, who's lyrics helped sculpt my cynical, ironic and some might say, slightly awkward personality. (Basically, it's anybody's fault but mine). Deal with it.

Joey Parkin is an eccentric with an eye for detail bordering on the obsessive. (Her other eye is just fine).

This book will appeal to the easily pleased, rarely offended and totally inept. It is written from life, imagination and complete fabrication.

Those lucky few with a blatant disregard for any form of political correctness, pompous formality or in fact anything even remotely boring will find it very entertaining and strangely alluring... a bit like Eddie Izzard in a frock. This little book is full of hidden surprises, ramblings and intrigue... so hold on to your gussets, you're in for a bumpy ride!

Ok, enough! just get on with it you tedious twerp!...

First things first...

Now before I go completely off on one, I need to tell you something about the nature of this book, how it came to be and what it is aiming to achieve, just to warn you, (in case you're hoping for gin recipes or a gripping mucky sub plot. It is not, I repeat not, a book for people with a perverse potato fetish or alcohol addiction as the front cover may suggest. Although...

You see I've had these thoughts and ideas since the age of four (my earliest memories) and have just collected them over time like people do with thimbles or those slightly disturbing stuffed, dead animals. Except mine are all rattling around in my (rather spacious) head, very much alive, growing by the day, right now... this very second and you are about to discover some rather disturbing aspects of my personality in thoughts which (in retrospect) should possibly have stayed right where they were! But it's too late now! They've escaped onto the pages of this very book laid bare for all to see (Oh matron!)

This book is however, a bit like a "forever" diary with my thoughts and events noted over decades rather than just a year at a time, as those transient, throwaway diaries tend to end their days propping up wonky tables (although this book could still be used for that purpose and many more outrageous pursuits!) Most are thrown on the scrap heap after just one year, replaced by a younger, much prettier version. Outrageous!

It's full of snippets, observations questions and assumptions, all laid bare to be dissected, chewed over, devoured and digested by you, the reader, hungry for entertainment, knowledge and humour! (No pressure then... just don't sue me ok?... pretty please?...) Suit yourself. Ok let's party!

Embarrassing moments..

This really is a true story I'm sorry to say and yes, it proves categorically I am a complete and utter numpty!...

Out shopping one fine and dandy day in Darwen Lancashire, I noticed there weren't many bespoke clothes stores so when I stumbled across one right on the main road, after several disappointing ones, in I trotted with a spring in my step.

I had time to kill so was in no rush, browsing away to my hearts' content. "Blimey, this is a posh shop" I foolishly thought as I rummaged through the rails of dresses and tops which all had protective cellophane over them to stop mucky fingers!

I could hardly contain my excitement at finding such a gem of a store when, like a bolt of lightening, I suddenly heard the rather impertinent lady behind the counter shout "Can I help you?" In a tone which better suited a bent high court judge! Undeterred, I carried on rummaging "no thanks, just looking..." as I briefly noticed a bus load of people gazing at me with bemused faces from outside the large window. "Erm, this IS a dry cleaners you know." Came the final crushing statement as my heart pounded and my face turned crimson.

The realization flashed across me... "quick brain! How do I get out of this one? Er, yes, I'm just checking something..." I mumbled as I skulked out past the bus stop trying to look like an official "dry cleaner inspector" and failing miserably. Shame I can't show my face around there anymore, I really liked Darwen....

More embarrassing moments...

Look admit it, when you get those weird little magazines through the door (no, not those!), aren't you the teeniest bit intrigued? I'm talking about those mags which advertise handy storage bags, shoe horns and well, there's no beating about the bush, I'll come straight out with it... "toe straighteners".

You see in my "youth" I danced a lot in 6" heels, hiked (ok. staggered) across golf courses and lanes with pot holes the size of the Grand Canyon, all in my stilettos just to look trendy and much, much taller. The result being my big toes are slightly bent and look a lot like pig's trotters.

Vanity perhaps? Well not really because dodgy toes can bring on bunions (just ask Posh spice) so I didn't want the same fate bestowed on me! I swiftly ordered them in a moment of weakness (I was most probably, in retrospect, on the verge of a breakdown). They sounded perfect, wear at night, no one would see them et voila! Ze toes of perfection! How did I know it would all end in chaos! They did look a lot like a I medieval torturing device but I thought, what do you expect for £5.99?

Oblivious to my impending fate I eventually got them on and attempted to climb the stairs to get some sleep. (The family by now were howling with laughter). Just you wait I thought As I lay there visualizing my nice straight toes I could hardly wait for morning.

Unfortunately, during the night I awoke with excruciating pain in both feet, confused and in agony, I fumbled in the dark trying to get to the light but the pain stopped me in my tracks. Dragging my contorted feet along the floor, I finally yanked the contraptions off my throbbing, swollen toes. If I hadn't woken up until morning I dread to think what carnage would have greeted me. (And I still walk like Danny La Rue on Crack!). Maybe just one more night...

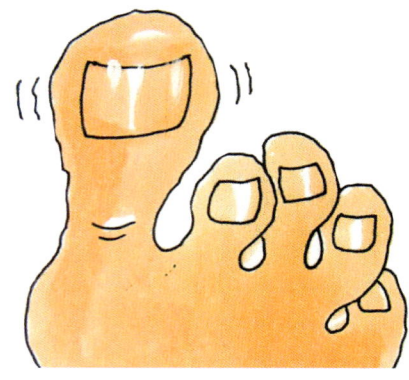

More embarrassing moments...

Optical illuSion...

On a recent trip to get my eyes checked I did a wonderful impersonation of Mr. Magoo (unintentionally of course!)

In the consultation room I read the notices with an unflattering air of confidence whilst moving from one contraption to the next so I moved along to the next chair facing what I assumed was yet another machine for testing my eyes.

I peered into it closer and closer but could not quite understand where I was supposed to rest my head so rested my chin on the top looking straight ahead waiting for instructions. It went eerily quiet so I slowly looked to the side whilst trying to keep my head still.

I noticed the poor woman optometrist trying to hold back a very obvious fit of laughter. After one of those really awkward moments she regained her composure to ask me to "please turn around from the photocopier!"

I immediately howled with laughter at my ridiculous antics and gave her permission to join in as the poor girl was about to explode!

It delayed our test as I couldn't see for tears! After what seemed an eternity, my test was complete and my result revealed I was PHOTOPHOBIC! (No, I love having my picture taken, I just have a sensitivity to light) which I already knew, as I scream like a vampire whenever a hint of light flashes before me!

Or, could it mean a sensitivity to photocopiers? I'm not sure, but I am sure I can never go back! Sooooo embarrassing.

D for don't go there!...

Don't mention the "D word". Dentists! Anyone who says they're painless or nothing to be scared senseless about is lying through their, well, teeth! They obviously have never been to any of mine or they are in complete denial due to their horrendous treatment no doubt.

I've had teeth drilled without any numbing, which have had abscesses behind them, jolting my whole body off the chair with such force I looked like Frankenstein's monster coming to life. (I also walked like him too for three days after!).

I've had excruciating fillings on teeth which have been numbed four times to prevent pain (oh really?) Still they won't believe me when I flinch in agony! Even a simple scale and polish ends up with a cut lip and severe bruising! And that's just the dentist! "Take that you over paid masochist!"

I've had enough of them making a fortune out of our misery and legalized torture! It's just like Guantanamo Bay in my practice. (Apart from the dress code). To top it all you get a whopping bill for the privilege and a reminder to "see you again in three weeks for a check up"... Dream on.

Oh, crumbs!

Posh restaurants! Now you've all been to places where you can bring your own wine, but this nouvelle quisine malarkey I encountered recently literally took the biscuit!

The food was so minimal they let you bring your own electron microscope! Tiny fragments of food, well I say food, it could have been dust for all I knew. Was it a starter? Surely not the main! I wasn't taking any chances. The whole "pudding" fitted on to one lousy spoonful so I was forced to lick the plate. I know this is unforgiveable but I was famished! (And the bill was pretty unforgiveable too!)

You know it's been a bad night when you get home from a meal out and have to raid the cornflakes!

The humble spud

Let's hear it for the humble spud
really boring to look at but doesn't half taste good!
peel it, boil it, mash it hard
but you'd better beware, be on your guard!
all's not well in Spudsville Tennessee
not good at all for you or me
coz spuds aren't just dumb and dented
they're getting clever, getting represented!
they've got veggie rights now, big ideas
got real attitude too and they've lost their fear!
It's no good smirking, they've turned real mean!
they're a crazy-eyed, badass fighting machine!
got their own lawyers and body-guards galore!
you just can't abuse them like that anymore!
they demand respect now, spuds are united!
you can only peel them if invited
so take care when grabbing a Jersey Royal
be gentle when you pull it from the soil
just keep it happy, calm and jolly
when you stuff it in your shopping trolley
and don't be disheartened, no, don't be sad!
not all our spuds turn bad
some are still kind and really quite nice
but if they look crazy-eyed, just opt for the rice!

TV embarrassing moments..

Is it just me or is there something a bit grotesquely intriguing about watching other people reveal their most intimate medical problems on TV? The programmes go out to millions of viewers so they must get people recognizing them in the street! "Hey! Didn't I see you on embarrassing illnesses? Dave the dodgy derrier isn't it? I recognise your bum off the telly, how is that weird fistula thingy getting on? Did you get it sorted? We got our HD telly just in the nick of time... cracking detail...".

Just when you think you've seen it all, someone turns up with the worst case of Athlete's foot ever! Like an explosion in a bakery! And one (lonely) bloke couldn't wait to drop his kecks to show us his very sore looking button mushroom! (We can't eat them any more!). To say "seen one you've seen them all" really doesn't wash once you've watched this. Just don't eat anything before, during or after this disturbing programme... ever again.

Annoying adverts: where do I start? I even wake myself up reciting "BOGOF!... I said you buy one, you get one free!" And during the day when I'm doing some banal task I start singing "Go compare!" in a bad italian accent. We're all being brain washed! (Or maybe I just need to watch less telly).

I've noticed men get a really raw deal in ads too. Take the 'Maltesers' bloke. His vindictive, evil wife's either burying his shirt in the garden, letting him drink rancid milk or throwing herself at the bloke next door! He just smiles dejectedly but inside he's seething and plotting his revenge... just you wait! I'm gonna take those Maltesers and stuff 'em somewhere where the sun never shines! And no, I don't mean Scotland!

The very last advert will be of him in a straight jacket, jailed for inflicting "death by chocolate" with the jaunty caption "Maltesers, so light you'll have to find other ways to be naughty".

Embarrassing parents!...

Why is it, when you go to visit your parents, you can only take really close family because you know they'll do or say something really embarrassing!... As soon as you turn up, your dad suddenly morphs into Jeremy Clarkson on crack! "Ey up... er what's mileage these days? What 's it like on petrol? Looks a right gas-guzzler that one! Which way did you come? Oh that's not t' quickest way, much slower going through Skipton.". And once the grade A cocaine's worn off he turns into Michael Fish!... "What's weather doing your way? Is it raining? Was it raining when you set off? What's the humidity like?... Pollen count? Should've gone t'other way like I said.

Once conversation inevitably grinds to a halt he plays his ace card. "Cuppa tea? ...how many sugars is it?" "NONE dad, never has been, never will be". But then he's nods off mid sentence dislodging his false teeth at the same time to resemble Butch off the Sooty show!

Growing up, you realize how different you are to your parent's when once upon a time the Christmas decorations were something to behold, a decorative wonderland of magical splendifference! Something to look forward to seeing from about October. Now I'm an official grown up, it just looks like Julian Clary's boudoir! (Not that I've had the pleasure). I'm torn between the simplicity of good design and the overwhelming urge to buy a musical, flashing santa gnome.

I think we should all do as we please and express our individuality but I can't help thinking the less the more. Then again it's amazing what you can do with a tribal head dress and a bag of spanners. Oh do as you like! (I need something to gawp at when I'm having an overpriced latte).

Torture I tell you...

Top Gear, again! (Yes I know it's a good programme with far too much emphasis on speed and mainly features cars you'll never get to drive in a million years!) but there's been so many repeats, you see Clarkson getting younger and younger then suddenly, wham! Aged thirty years overnight! Ouch! It's bad enough seeing him in those skanky jeans and tucked-in shirt but do they have to freak us out like that? And what's happening with Hammond's hair? Freaky, plain freaky. At least put a warning on like you do for flash photography!

Keep it down!

Not only do I hate smells but also noise! Unnecessary noise, TV noise especially! Now I love my telly but why do adverts have to be on three times the volume? I've adjusted it so often I've acquired a sixth sense of when an advert break is about to come up! "Grasshopper, It's time to pick up the remote..." But how will I know master?" "You will know"... "Oh Thank you master, you have taught me well".

Big Bruvva. Ah, it's over at last. I'm gonna miss hours of endless cheap, boring telly watching nobodies arguing, flashing their falsies, swearing and lazing about in squalor. All that wit, deep conversation and insight... where was it? Sylvester Stallone's mum was the only bit I ever liked, just her, the rest was just...

(Imagine a Geordie accent)...

"Three fifteen A.M.... The housemates are all comatosed apart from Zak who's slumped in the kitchen trying to butter some toast with his knuckles... Three hours later, Jemmima is in the garden plucking her nasal hair with a pair of skanky tweezers she found in a tramp's vest."

"Letitia is in the bathroom mumbling and foaming at the mouth. Must be brushing her teeth... ah, now she's on the floor twitching n' body poppin'. She loves to be the centre of attention does Letitia. Her flared nostrils and bulging eyes look proper smashin'!"

Join the queue...

Phone rage! No wonder people are losing it. Queues, queues and more queues! You rarely speak to a human anymore, automated everything..

Dling, dling... Thank you for calling "waiting for death". Please select your preference: Dial one for "I just want to talk to a real human being", two for "I'm totally losing the will to live now" or three for "Oh forget it I'll just hang myself".

We should make queueing an olympic event:

In the first lane we have Dotty from Wetherby (in a psychedelic floral rain mac)... "Is it Thursday yet luvvie?" In the second lane, Luke from London (well dressed, high achiever, impatient professional) "This is totally outrageous! I'm calling my lawyer Justin right now!". In lane three we have: Johnathan from Harrogate (tanned and trendy fitness junkie, all in spandex) "Ill have the mocha, chocca half de-caffe triple mocha for quite a lotta, over easy, lemon squeezy." And in lane four, Stan from Blackburn: (No frills builder) "And I'll just stand 'ere n' rant coz ther's no way on this earth 'am payin' that! Just give us a packet o' crisps you robbin' cheapskates! Cheers luv".

And so it goes. I'm so used to queueing now I just join any I see, regardless! I can go for days without eating or sleeping. In fact I'd give Jesus a run for his money! Forty days and forty nights?... Piece 'o cake!

Our local shopping precinct looks like "dawn of the dead" come January sales! Hordes of over fed, under exercised hopefuls slowly shuffling along with their bulging bags of tat! We Brits were born to queue!

Queueing for gold

Queues and automated attitude!

Don't people queue really untidily? Or is it just me? I'd just squeezed into the chippy last July as it was freezing outside and just three people in the queue so I asked them to move up a bit... well, you'd have thought I'd asked them to donate a kidney! Should have seen their shocked bloated faces! Haven't they heard of queue management? No spacial awareness some folk! All I wanted was an orderly snake formation and the door shut. Is that too much to ask?

So you're in a queue and only got two seconds left on your car parking and suddenly find yourself behind a coach party from Cleckheaton on a mystery tour! (The mystery being what the hell are they all doing in HMV high on caffeine and sugar?...)

You finally get to the till with your must have "two for one" bargain T-shirt only to be served by "Egor" from the York Dungeon! Avoiding eye contact he asks (in a gurgling, gasping for air kind of way) "would you like a Toblerone... on offer today? Or a... book of stamps? Batteries? How about a cream egg?... or a special limited edition photo of my belly button? "Er, no thanks" I reply, slowly, "I'd just like my change and the will to live". But then he looks right at you, crushed, in a "who killed my kitten?" kind of way and makes you feel like Cruella Deville!

You have to get a way, fast, you know you're up for a £40 stitch up as soon as you get to your car, but no... there's the barrage of street sellers and entertainers to dodge next and you're not even sure if you even want the ruddy T-shirts now!

Those were the days!

My school days weren't exactly the best years of my life. At junior school I was called to the front of the whole school as we lined up in our various classes in the playground each morning ready to march in. I had been caught chatting as we stood, arms on each others shoulders in perfect lines. I must have been around six or seven and I'll never forget it.

A very crabby teacher oredered me to the front of the whole school and held my arms up with one hand then proceeded to slap my legs with all her might. It was a chilly day and those smacks stung hard. She continued slapping. I tried to dodge them by doing a strange variation of "River dance" but to no avail.

Suddenly I peed all over her scratchy, bony hand. The place went silent for a while until she finally stopped and just ordered me back in line (along with my soaking kecks). I slowly squelched back, stinking of pee, looking just like John Wayne after eight months in the saddle! (But not quite as tall). St. Cuthbert's Primary, Darwen, Lancashire. Thanks for that. I do hope your policies on child abuse have now been reformed.

That was just primary school, where I used to turn up really early just to swap the chairs around in my classroom as I was convinced all the brainy kids had magic chairs. How else could they correctly answer questions on history or recite the nine times tables?

They had to be magic chairs! There was no other logical explanation. Once swapped, I sat confidently awaiting the teacher's challenge but recoiled in horror when I realised it didn't work as I sat there dumfounded. Even then I thought it must only work for the people who's chair it truly was, not, a naughty imposter such as myself!

Just you wait!

Secondary school left me scarred too, in more ways than one. Firstly, my thoughtful, caring sister who was just two years older than my good self had spent those two years telling all the violent, psycho kids who were trying to bully her to "keep away, coz my sister's coming next term and she'll GET you! She's well hard and she'll have the lot of you! Just you wait." And they did.

Thanks for that. You guessed it, when I joined "big school" they were all after me, boys too! (And not in a "kiss catch" kind of way either!) So I had to get tough quick or I wouldn't survive. We had no anti-bullying policies in those days so I made a point of being the scruffiest, meanest, most crazy faced weirdo I could (with amazing ease) and it worked! They didn't know how to take me, hadn't a clue how "crazy" I could be and only the absolute elite kids ever tried to find out.

Way before the days of "Mad Max" I'd just do bizarre random acts whenever threatened just to get a reaction and scare them into leaving well alone. After all, who wants to hang around someone with scrunched up crisp packets stuffed up their nose, chomping grass? They've obviously got enough problems of their own.

I soon made lots of friends as I was entertaining if nothing else so it wasn't all bad. My eccentric sense of humour seemed to go down a treat, imitating the teachers and drawing them on the board just before lesson gave me a great insight into identifying characters and a life long fascination for people watching. However, it doesn't pay too well. Ho hum.

(Ho hum? Who on earth says that these days?) Just me then.

Heads you lose!

My deranged, evil English teacher really took a shine to me (not in a good way). Hurling a wooden dust board wiper was nothing new but today was special. Quietly seated at our tatty desks, we followed the story as selected kids read out various chapters and to add a little spice to this rather tedious exercise I decided to follow it upside down (not me, the book). I was still paying attention and carefully following it (as my method took far more concentration) when I was rudely interrupted by a random and totally insane act of violence by this monster.

Suddenly I felt this enormous crack on my head which stunned me for a few seconds. He'd sneaked over to me and used the full force of the hard backed book (yes it would be wouldn't it?) plus his own, to maximum effect! Thud!

The reading immediately stopped as the sound was rather sickening and the whole back row awoke in silence. I turned crimson, grimaced and turned my book around slowly without looking at his face, in total agony, my head throbbing, eyes stinging and my heart racing. (I was familiar with anxiety induced panic attacks but luckily my epic pride can override anything) so I didn't let on, determined not to feed his inflated ego.

The whole room knew he'd gone too far. I just wish I'd got up and done the same to him then reported him to the head or social services but you just didn't in those days, couldn't, as you'd risk another crack for your trouble. Hurrah for Childline!

He died just a few months later but it had nothing to do with the evil curse I'd put on him for his lousy, unforgivable actions. Honest!

All you'll ever need to know about...

MATHS: Just buy a calculator

ENGLISH: Shakespeare's over rated and dead, read something else.

CHEMISTRY: A bunsen burner & your facial hair will soon meet

BIOLOGY: Everything steals energy from other things to survive. (Usually by devouring). It's messy and can get very ugly.

GEOGRAPHY: Buy a submarine with Sat-Nav. It's gonna get wet.

MUSIC: You do not sound like you think you sound.

SOCIOLOGY: Human nature stinks, trust nobody, not even yourself.

RELIGIOUS STUDY: Think for yourself.

SPORT: There's always someone faster and stronger than you.

GRAPHICS: The less the more.

HISTORY: There's a great clue in the title. Move on.

FRENCH: They all speak excellent English.

COOKERY: It's far cheaper and much nicer to eat out.

ART: Your teacher is a drunk. You're on your own.

PHYSICS: What goes up doesn't always come down.

SCIENCE: There's no such thing as a fact. Question EVERYTHING.

PHILOSOPHY: You may as well ask the dog.

PSYCHOLOGY: Everyone else is mad but you.
        (& if the dog answers you back, it's game over!)

Soooooo annoying!

Phone text messages!
Why, oh why do they all sound like Stephen Hawkins? "THIS IS A TEXT MESSSAGING SYSTEM FROM 0...2...4...4..5...6..7..8.... FOR ... JO...EY PAR...KIN.... YOU HAVE THE CHAR...ISMA OF A SMALL... LAND MAM...MAL... AND... A VER...RY... INSIG...NIFI...CANT ONE... AT...THAT...

You'd think by now we could have a proper human voice! Even Stephen could have one but he chooses to keep his well known Darlek one (it's his choice). He's too busy looking for black holes to worry anyway. I find 'em on a daily basis.... especially in my purse, where my cash weirdly vanishes into massless (or should I say cashless) particles at an amazing rate! Work that one out Stevie!

CHEESE!
Why is cheese so ruddy expensive? It's complete and utter madness! And obviously a conspiracy. Cheese is loaded with fat (usually two thirds!) and the rest is mouldy milk leftovers! Come on, come clean all you cheese producers!
You must stop milking it! (Sorry). Stop creaming off the poor, unsuspecting general public (can't help myself) and please charge a reasonable amount for a wedge of cheese. (About twenty pence should cover it, you thieving gets). And don't even get me started on mushrooms!

Global warming?
Anyone with an ounce of grey matter should realize the planet is constantly changing, freezing, heating up, expanding, moving, bending, shaking... it's called evolution, deal with it. We inhabit a big gassy cluster of chemicals so stop blaming it all on farting cows and the Chinese. Let's face up to the wider issues of why there are STILL plastic bags in production. (I'm so angry I could crush a grape! (An organic one obviously).

Those people?
Who turn statements into questions? Like I just did? It's so ruddy annoying and a travesty of the great English language? Everything is a ruddy question? And now everybody seems to be doing it? Even me? No, I refuse, point blank. Stop it! Stop it now? I'm warning you? Doh!

BIG night out? Just say no!

You've got a big night out planned with your girlie mates and the clock is ticking! (In more ways thatn one). So what the hell do you wear these days? It was nineteen eighty seven when you last got dressed up to go out on the razzle and now you've hit forty plus (age, not waist size, well not quite) nothing looks or feels right. Only one thing to do! Get the music on and lock the door.

Turn the music up... party down! Burn baby burn, disco inferno, burn that mamma down! It's 1985 "yeah baby!" You start moving to the groove, you turn the volume up, start feeeling like you're eighteen again, you grab your wackiest outfit, looks fab! You keep on dancin' as your confidence soars! It's 9pm already so you grab your coat and head for the bus. "Bring it on! Let's party!" Trouble is you've forgotten you can no longer walk in anything higher than your slippers and it's minus five out there.

You stagger to the bus stop looking like Danny La Rue on crack in your sequined micro mini dress (which rolled right up with every step due to static so your fake fur g-string all but disappeared into your tightly clenched buttocks! It's so damn cold your mascara has snapped off as you blinked and still no bloody bus! You try and text your mates but they're all tanked up on Lambrini and don't even know which pub they're in. Your bunions are throbbing, your face is swollen due to the howling wind and you're losing the will to live. You attempt to walk into town but your feet are like numb pig's trotters, your hair is exploding, your'e paralysed with cold and... there goes your bus.

What on earth were you thinking? Get home right now you complete numpty and have a hot bath, telly on and a bowl of Cornflakes. It's not 1985, it's not big and it's not clever. Next time just say no.

Top tips for under ten bob... (50p)!

Teeth whitening, for that celebrity smile!
Want to impress on that first hot date? Simply stick white chewing gum over your wonky, decaying stumps and smile away! You'll have fresh breath confidence too (at least until the curry) so it's a win win situation!

Want to live in a palace? But you live in a bum hole?
Why simply hang tiny minature chandaliers from your eyelashes and every room will look palatial darling!

Want to look intelligent but you're as thick as sh*te?
Simply comb your fringe up with extra strong gel and shave off your eyebrows. Your forehead will now appear so big everyone will treat you with the respect you deserve.

Movie star looks?
Simply stay up all night, get loads of tattoos, (which you'll regret when dumped), stick a pair of large sunglasses on, moan a lot and dress like a hobbit, job done.

Want to look like Lady Gaga?
Simply wrap some parma ham (or luncheon meat if you're northern) around your middle, lock the dog in the garage, borrow some authopeidic shoes and practice "the claw". If you already have arthritic hands, you are a natural.

Want Sky TV?
Simply glue a wok to the side of the house and be bang up to date with the neighbours! What? You can't get the latest blockbuster on a wok? Perfect, you can't on Sky either! (Alledgedly!)

Want to drive a Rolls Royce?
Simply cellotape a foil cat onto the bonnet of your Morris Minor and put some "walnut effect" sticky back plastic onto the dashboard. Place a big cushion on your driver seat and drive slowly with a smug look.

Dance like Michael Flatley?
Really? Ok, simply set fire to your shoes (preferably when you're wearing them) and you'll be River dancing in no time.

Rants in their pants!

Blokes!
Blokes can build space ships, solve complex equasions, do sudoku and even remove monster spiders on request so why, oh why, can't they ever find anything? Ask them to get the cellotape from the kitchen drawer and they're completely flumaxed! "Eh? Where? Not 'ere, definitely not 'ere.. nope". You get up from your eighteen multi-tasking jobs and open the same drawer to find it immediately.
(It's one of the great mysteries of the universe).

Women (See how fair I am?)
Women have a lot of skills, obviously, but there's one really awful, cringeingly vile habit some of them have which I must mention. When they meet each other they shriek at the top of their ear piercing voices much to the annoyance of people within a 10 mile radius. Dogs howl, birds fly off course, glasses shatter and I have to cover my lug holes before I blow a gasket. Come on girls, just tone it down a bit will you? Hug fine, witchy screech, not fine.

Foot Spa's!
HOW could anyone possibly think they were anything but unhygienic swamps of festering gunk? I saw people sat right in the salon window sipping cheap champagne as tiny fish munched on their corns whilst pooping. (Not the people, the fish... mainly). It's not a good look.

Bottled water? What next?
Why in the name of Jesus H. Samuel would any sane human being spend money on bottled water? It's got more bacteria than Synthia Pain's underpants!

Totally unecessary, just like buying bottled air! (Unless of course you happen to live with someone with a recurring bowel disorder or a passion for sprouts!) Both? Ok there are exceptions! I feel your pain.

Ready sliced vegetables!
I despair. Look, we all like a few luxuries in life but this really is ridiculous! If I was the richest person alive I would not buy ready sliced veg. (I'd get my butler to do it obviously!) Life may be too short to stuff a mushroom but slicing your own veg takes seconds. What next? Ready buttered bread?... Ready gnarled pies?... Intravenous chips? ... somebody stop me!

Faith, hope and charity...

Charity shops... "thrift" shops, second hand stores... they always smell of moth balls and damp gussets! There's one every other shop in Harrogate (obviously slightly posher than other Northern towns) as here you can actually *fold* the underpants! (Fear not, even I draw the line at purchasing second hand undies!)

And what a cheek these days! Their donated clothes are nearly as expensive as the new stuff! If I spot a skanky jumper for more than £3 I think "grabbing, thieving, robbing gets!" (I daren't tell you what I think if it's a fiver!).

I love a bargain and "retro" clothes but especially enjoy the element of surprise! Plus it's the perfect place for a tight fisted, scruffy old shyster like my good self! Where else can you (legally) spend hours loitering about with absolutely no intention of paying more than £3, fumbling through a sea of tatty paraphernalia whilst keeping warm and listening to the jaunty banter of Stray FM?... Ok. apart from TK Max.

Now I don't hate fashion, just the "I must keep up with what everyone else is wearing" mentality. Why on earth would you pay to look very similar to someone else, then chuck it a month later coz "it's so last season"? Eh?

Come on, we can do much better than that! It's really unethical and very wasteful. Worse still, highly unimaginative. (Although I am addicted to "project runway"). If I find I'm wearing anything remotely fashionable or trendy it is purely by accident.

Definition of the word BARGAIN: A piece of tat you don't really want which, if you buy two of, somehow seems to justify the price! (Well it works for me!).

Smells like a bargain!...

I'm thrifty n' nifty with a nose for a sale!
I can sniff out a bargain in a force nine gale!
I spend three pound fifty on makeup job done
I've a face like a bull dog licking it's bum
I eat what I like and wear what I choose
I walk everywhere and lay off the booze

As for shopping I don't spend a lot
I don't follow fashion, I like what I've got
"This season's must haves" for shopping junkies
Get a life, It's fun when you couldn't give a monkey's
I rummage in thrift shops for treats and surprises
It's such a buzz when your blood pressure rises

Discarded clothes needing love and care
but avoid the second hand underwear!
Don't waste your money on designer tat
just design your own!... customize that!
Don't follow the herd, you'll get constipated
Be individual, intriguing and liberated!

If the thought of buying dead people's clothing appalls
and you can't quite stomach the whiff of moth balls
take solace because not all of these stores are manky
just don't go in without your gas mask or hanky!

Join the revolution!..

We should start an original clothing revolution! Right now! And eradicate this evil practice once and for all! Let's customize our own gear! Re-style, re-invent and swap stuff! How much fun would that be? And it would cost peanuts!

Let's make it trendy to be original! Make it nerdy to wear designer labels, we are free thinkers not sheep! We're all designers! So join me in my crusade to flaunt our originality and differences! Wallow in our uniqueness! Bask in our unadulterated creativity! OK then... I'll get my coat.

Have we have become a nation of self obsessed loners? I ask this because I'm sat at my state of the art iMac googling "teeth whitening on a pittance" having just photoshopped my pearly greys on a recent photo and amazed myself at the difference! (If only I'd put the tea on instead! I wouldn't be in this pickle!). It's not that I really need it, I spend seventy percent of my life in a virtual stupor where I don't see anyone I need to impress so why the compulsion for white teeth?

Must have been that shiny photo of beaming Melinda Messinger that finally tipped me over the edge, maybe I should just lay off the computer for a while and take up guerning... or just stick to reading the Dandy.

In just a few clicks I'd neatened, tweaked and transformed myself from a dull toothed troglodite into a gleaming toothpaste model! If only it was that simple (and that cheap!)

I've also stuck paper across my teeth just to see how white they could go but I just looked like a boxer.

I Don't...

I don't drink, don't smoke, don't do as I'm told
I don't dress for my age coz I just don't feel old
I don't like to sit still, there's so much I can do
life's full of surprises when every day's new

I don't like to blend in or follow the masses
& I hate to admit it but I really need glasses
I don't do as I should, I do things my way
I go roller-blading and clubbing on Friday

I don't waste my time knitting, I'd rather have fun days!
I don't darn socks or go to church Sundays
I don't need forgiveness, no need for redemption
growing old disgracefully is my sole intention

I don't fear a thing, wouldn't hurt a fly
I'm proud to be me and I just don't see why
people assume I'm just a middle aged mum
but I've got a wild streak and there's far worse to come!

Soap... nothing but soap...

Is it just me or has anyone else thought it strange that there are now shops which sell soap, nothing else just soap! Millions of shapes, styles, colours and scents but come on! Soap? It's just weird... even for an obsessive compulsive like me it's a little over the top! (I do like the neat rows and colour coding though!)

Let me get this right. A shop... that sells soap... just soap, the whole soap and nothing but the soap. Can anyone *be* that filthy? How on earth do they make a living? I worry about these things.

Shopping used to be fun in the days when we had streets and daylight, now it's all squished together in giant malls under florescent lights! Fighting your way through hordes of lunatics hell bent on spending as much as possible even if it's only to justify the extortionate parking fees! There's nothing worse than paying a fiver to end up window shopping. (Unless of course it's windows you were after).

Shop on line in comfort with a nice cuppa and a packet of Hobby nobs! it's so much easier! Too easy in fact! You see it, you click it bigger, you click it, you like it, oops! You just bought it! Then it arrives unexpected a couple of days later when you were hoping it was all just a bad dream.

The amount of things we've forgotten we'd bought... It's like Christmas day every day in our house! (What we're supposed to do with that rocket launcher we got off that funny looking "Algae zebra" website I've no idea! There's nowhere for the batteries for one thing).

Stupid trousers!

Stupid trousers!... Is it just me or do most trousers lack the top half? I'm permanently pulling them up over my escaping bum then pulling down my extra long t-shirt (which had to be specifically purchased to accompany the trousers making all my other t-shirts redundant!)

I now have to hang them in a separate wardrobe to avoid antagonizing stares, hate mail and abuse from all the t-shirts left jobless and bitter.

Still my bum escapes because there is nothing holding it in! Stupid trousers, they defy gravity, the zip's half the length of a normal one and bending down to pick anything up is simply not an option.

Of course I forget and try to reach for s o m e t h i n g, to be met with howls of laughter, gasps of disgust and disapproving faces, you guessed it, my bum's escaped again and my kecks are on display, looking like an explosion in a muffin shop! I'm becoming a flasher.

The only thing that could find me remotely attractive at that point is a wayward baboon or Russell Brand, obviously!

Join my campaign to bring back proper t r o u s e r s!
Nice roomy one's such as jodhpurs which can easily store a large frozen chicken without detection like in the good old days! "They just don't make them like they used to!"... And where's the fun in that?

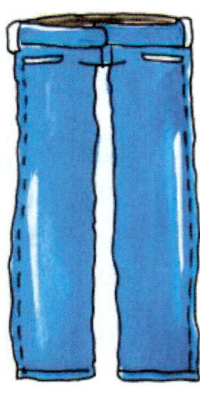

Grandad!... Not again!...

I caught him red handed, just about to mug her!
A defenseless little lady, the spineless bugger!
I dragged him away looking all coquettish
tried to explain he'd a chronic shoe fetish!

I'm not 'avin that, he's been done twice before
loitering with intent on this very shop floor!
I remember it well, he was clutching a mule,
got fined £50 quid the silly old fool!

He's got form he has, he's no goody goody
He's a badass grandad and he's wearing a hoodie!
Say wot you like you're gonna get done
You can't go round doing that just for fun!

She'll probably press charges n' who can blame her?
Stop staring at my feet, no you can't 'av my trainer!
Whadaya mean it's for your private collection?
Get back 'ere now for your own protection!

We've had enough of weirdo's like you
Fondling ladies ankles and nicking their shoe!
Get a proper hobby 'n stick just to Sundays
(When the missus pops out 'n you can try on her undies!)

Fon-ruddy-don't!

Who in their right mind would willingly invite eight ravenous people over to sit around a single solitary bowl of runny cheese, the temperature of the sun, armed only with a long tiny fork which belongs to "the Borrowers" and a clump of stale bread? The word fondue and party should never be used in the same context ever, just like "royalty" with "outdated" - no wait a minute, that kind of works!

Fondue? Fon-ruddy don't! One glowing red hot bowl, full of bubbling cheese... urgh, I feel ill just thinking of it. Whatever possesses people to even consider that a good idea?

Let's all sit around this sorry looking red hot bowl full of molten lava to suffer third degree burns trying to eat it while our lips get welded to the fork (which, by the way, we all share!) So we'll instantly lose all sensation in our mouths for a few months and put on 3 stone overnight. Yes, that'll work.

Thankfully they're now out of fashion! Let's hope it's for good! Chuck 'em in the cupboard along with your bread maker, foot spa and all the other useless items we "couldn't do without!"

That reminds me, last time I ever went to a fondue "party" I ended up next to a guy with a horrendous nasal problem who spent the whole time snorting and slurping! Urggh! ...Took us eighteen hours to finish that ruddy bowl!

Remember kids... just say "NO!"

Sweet as candy...

I'm a bit of a foodie I admit. I've tried loads of restaurants, cafes, good , bad and downright dangerous and it's made me very critical. So bad in fact I think I've got what can only be described as "gastronomical tourrettes!" Just can't help myself. "The custard to pudding ratio here is totally wrong". The amount of times I've had to ask for more custard you wouldn't believe! Come on chefs, sod this nouvelle cuisine rubbish and give us more custard! NOW!

As for presentation, well it can make or break a good meal. (I watch a lot of Master Chef!) But even I draw the line at that frothy stuff they keep putting all over the plate which looks like cuckoo spit! Either that or the chef really can't take my constructive criticism!

I vividly recall congratulating myself for devouring a full family sized packet of salted peanuts whilst watching the original King Kong! Must have been a billion calories and enough salt to bring on a stroke but hey, I was young!

And devouring a full packet of custard creams was a sinch! Dipped in a hot cup of tea obviously! We ate jelly straight from the pack, chocolate galore and always ended our meal with a cheese and jam butty (even if the meal itself was a cheese and jam butty!) Oh those hazy sugary days! Yes we were hyper, yes we had violent mood swings and attention deficit disorders! Yes we ran amock like wild animals but we were never bored!

I'm still weaning myself off the white stuff but once a sugar junkie always a sugar junkie... and I've got the dentist bills to prove it!

Nothing sweet about that!

Stinks! Has anyone ever gone into a place and had to run straight out before they barfed? If you're sensitive to smells you'll know what I mean. I was out with the family and we strolled into a gorgeous olde worlde sweet shop which must have had a recent flood as I was met with a wall of stench!

As soon as I got in I had to get out. I'm not exaggerating here but it stunk like the decaying undergarments of a recently unearthed bog monster from a long lost civilization of mutant boglodites who worshipped all things boggy and rotten! Damp and dark yet strangely alluring... I had to make a sudden bolt for the door (and I don't mean in a foundry kind of way either!)

Holding my breath, I was astounded to see other people behaving as if nothing untowards was happening, oblivious to the gut wrenching stench which apparently only I was aware of! I know we were in chocolate nirvana but even so, I had to get out! Once outside I gasped for air as I regained full consciousness. And as I waited for the rest of the family, I considered these three slightly worrying possibilities...

A. I have a super human sense of smell. (Could be).
B. My brain is trying to trick me so I won't buy any more sweets or chocolate after years of sugar abuse. (Quite possibly).
Or C. (And this one really is worrying!)... I AM THE BOG MONSTER!

Luckily they had indeed suffered a flood but were not as sensitive to the stench as I was so I guess I must have super human powers! But why couldn't I have the ability to become invisible instead? Typical.

Absolutely typical!

Sugar butties & near death by chocolate!...

Is it just me or has anyone else tried the culinary delight of the sugar butty? (It's like eating a sand sandwich!) Grinding the sweet grains as you savour the cheap margarine and doughy white bread... To say we ate junk food in the 70's & 80's is an understatement of the century!

Every Saturday when I was young I'd rush back from the supermarket clutching a box of "bird's Trifle" meant for four people (no it wasn't meant for extremely spoilt budgies!) which my sister and I made as fast as possible without waiting for it to set properly just to sprinkle on the hundreds and thousands which spilt everywhere! Then we'd woof the lot down between us!... Happy days!

As for chocolate, lovely, smooth, milky, delectable chocolate, it should carry a health warning! I'm still having flashbacks from my very own "scrap heap challenge" moment...

I was nine years old waiting in dad's car at the scrap yard while he rummaged around for a back light indicator for his Capri ghia... I decided to eat my chocolate cream egg as I was getting bored and to add a little intrigue to this rather familiar exercise I decided to cram the lot into my mouth to see if it would go. It went alright! It lodged behind my teeth !

Half laughing, half panicking in the mirror I breathed in and literally started to choke as the gloopy egg lodged in my windpipe! I froze, went purple, gasped for air and made bone-chilling noises usually only heard on horror films like "Saw" or from a constipated donkey! No-one around to help, it really could have been "death by chocolate" but I guessed there were far worse ways to go!

Luckily my heart was strong and I finally recovered after a few agonising minutes! Dad finally returned none the wiser with his bounty (not the chocolate kind!) And I sat there exhausted giving chocolate cream eggs the respect they so rightly deserve. "How *do* you eat yours?"

I scream...

How come ice cream vans haven't been "done" by the noise abatement society? Talk about noise pollution! If I was to drive around every cul-de-sac blasting out Marilyn Manson there'd be uproar!... I did try it once. I even handed out rotting carcasses and sheep's entrails but they weren't impressed. Kids today eh? It's one rule for one...

How come they haven't been done by the trade's description act either? You see a giant 99 the size of, well, a giant and what do you get? A tiny ice cream straight from, you guessed it, " The Borrowers" kitchen! How do they get away with it? I know size isn't everything but really! Now Ripley, they do know how to make ice cream... (If you're reading this I love the mint choc!) Shameless I tell you.

One of my best ever icy creamy sensation moments was at St. Ives in Cornwall The kids had just got a lemon meringue flavoured one with bubblegum and peardrop bits on top which, when I stole a lick, (I say lick coz I can't bite them without bringing on a seizure) tasted amazing! Not like any other ice cream I'd ever tasted and one I would definitely risk searing nerve pain for any day. And as I'm weirdly sensitive to everything that's no mean feat!

I made a mental note of where we got them so we could pop in on the way back along the front and I'd get one all to my little greedy self. Unfortunately, due to my complete lack of directional sense we asked in several shops but couldn't locate "the one". I vowed to go back and find it one day even if I have to try every store!... (Well someone's got to).

Really annoying friends!...

Slow talkers! Yikes, I get the urge to ram a bumper pack of laxatives up their jacksy just to hurry things up a little! Now you might think that's a little bit extreme (and it is) but you haven't met my friend "Spitty Sue" (O.K. you know I can't use her real name but maybe it's a double bluff).

She has a first class honours degree in boring the pants off people! Not only does she speak sooooo slowly and laboured, adding totally irrelevant detail to every tale.... (takes hours to describe her post code!) You know the type: "Yeah... Henry and... who's his friend? Now I do know the name as I remember writing it down on my lovely floral note book which I got for..." Still awake?... (three days later)... "oh yah, Michael Johnson, or was it Jameson? ..." Oh somebody save me!

She also SPITS buckets every time she speaks, oblivious to the worrying amount of her own phlegm building up on MY face as she always gets just a little too close.

I also find myself filling in the tedious gaps and pauses in her droning explanations: "yeah... we're thinking of buying a th.. er... em.. .
a..." Thesbian?
"No, no.. a..."
A thoroughly dangerous heat seeking missile?
"No, no course not ..."
A thoughtful pigmy with a lisp?
"Now don't be silly..."
Until I eventually grab my car keys and leg it.

So annoying! (Maybe it's me who just needs to slow down... no, surely not). And no, I can't drop her! Why? Coz she's got a ski chalet in Verbier.
That's why!

More really annoying friends!...

Then there's Sonia, who talks about herself, constantly and worse, if you cunningly try to change the conversation she turns it straight back to her... "You've been ill? I was really ill last week... (by now I've glazed over and start planning my next holiday, meal, murder...).

Then there's Jess (of course it's not her real name!), who's as tight as a duck's bum! Never gets the drinks in first and when it's her turn she's nowhere to be seen. Never has enough for the taxi, yet spends all night showing off her latest designer tat!... Handbags, jewellery... Zzz "boring alert!".

So when people like this never change, just put a note in your address book or diary to spend as little time with them as necessary!

It's very liberating to de-clutter your social life! Just think of the great times ahead with people you enjoy who don't suck every ounce of life out of you! Your time is precious so spend it wisely grasshopper and you will have the secret to true happiness.

Obsessive friends are a pain too unless they're obsessed about showering you with gorgeous prezzies (as if that ever happens!) But OCD doesn't have to be all bad. I have been known to be overly obsessive, even compulsive or as I like to call it... Tidy. So what if I can't stand clutter? Hate things out of place or wonky pictures? I think of it more as attention to detail.

OK. I'm not a severe case and I do draw the line at checking the front door eighty times but it does have it's good points... You're never mucky, you rarely get burgled as you've checked everything a million times and your home's always ready for a visit from the Queen.

"We are not amused"

Unbe-ruddy-lievable!

Once upon a time, in a land not too far away, I went for a night out in Newcastle with my Geordie mate to a trendy nightclub where she immediately got her shoe nicked right off her foot!

Some strange bloke just ran up and snatched it! We thought he was just joking and assumed he'd return in a few minutes. You guessed it, not a chance. Couldn't see him for dust.

It was a sparkly flip flop so what on earth could he want with that? The mind boggles. Maybe he had a weird flip flop fetish (try saying that after a few pints!) Probably just wanted to add it to his bespoke collection! If people can enjoy collecting crisp packets then anything's possible.

We spent the rest of the evening searching in bins and under tables in the futile hope of spotting it. You could tell by the disgusted expressions that people assumed we were vagabonds trying to find fag ends or bits of discarded food!

(We did find some rather unusual items but that's another story).

My night's out just never go according to plan, I still wonder if that shoe pinching weirdo had a glass cabinet at home in his living room with itemized shoes and accessories all colour coded and in date order!

At least he didn't collect shrunken heads!.. That would just be creepy! All those shrunken eyes staring out from a glass cabinet! (Do shrunken heads have shrunken eyes or do the eyes stay the same size? Because if they did, they'd all look like Pete Dockerty! ... No, that's just too weird!

More faces than t'town hall clock!

Aren't some women really two-faced? And they're so good at it, so convincing they should get national recognition awards.... "Hi Babes, look at you! Where did ya get your hair done it looks sensational? Must have cost a fortune! Just stunning, can I have a feel? Oh, gorgeous..." And you guessed it, as soon as she leaves the room... "Who in the name of Jehosserfats, gets their hair done like that? What does she think she looks like? I've seen better looking hair on a tramp's wart! "

Human behaviour, isn't it fascinating? Take rudeness for instance... I was in the dining room of a house we were thinking of buying and as it was a dull day merely asked if it got much light (due to the trees and shrubs outside the window) and the snotty cow replied "if we want sun we go to Spain" to which I replied "hey, that's a coincidence! We go there too! But only when we want the sh*ts!". Pardon my french but she was asking for it... big time! (Yes we still bought the house).

Weather warning... boring alert!

What's our obsession with the weather? I think it's all just a front (and not a warm one) to cover the fact that most of us have bugger all else to talk about. Brrr, isn't it freezing? I just can't get warm. Is it me or is it chilly in here? Must be t' coldest winter since the great winter of 79 or the big freeze of 82...."

Why can't TV weather reports be a little more exciting? They could at least wear a funny hat to match the impending downpour to add a bit of intrigue and dare I say humour.

So next time you feel a mundane weather comment about to burst out, try changing it to something more useful such as "sale on at Argos, starts Tuesday! (But obviously only if this is true as it's embarrassing enough going there when there's no sale!) That's if you know anyone who admits to shopping there. I do. I have no shame (or taste some might add!) But I love a bargain! Bring it on!

Looks like rain.

Merry whatever!...

Weird Christmas isn't it? Especially when you're not religious! "Happy holiday" really isn't getting into the swing of things is it? But what a great excuse to get lots of presents. Even if they are naff. I love the element of surprise, coz that's usually the best bit.

A bunch of famished strangers turn up at your front door calling themselves "family" but you only have their word for it and settle down on your sofa for the best part of 3 days! Occasionally moving for the odd bottom burp or the lure of yet another mince pie! They eat you out of house and home then clear off when the whisky runs out. It passes the time though when all the repeats are on and everything's shut, apart from the fridge.

Then there's the embarrassing present opening! I could win an Oscar for the performances I give to look genuinely impressed! "It's really nice thanks. Really. Yeah, I like that." Their eager eyes still piercing yours, searching for the giveaway smirk or nervous twitch. "No, really, it's lovely, cheers". Silence. I much prefer silly presents which have had a bit of thought such as anything home made, a poem or a drawing of me in a bad mood... That's what I really like! Let's boycott all tedious predictable gifts and get back to the good old days of making your own!... (Unless of course, it's a Bugatti Veyron, a giant Toblerone or a micro piglet in a pink scarf).

And why on earth do we celebrate Birthdays? Must be a marketing scam. You're a whole year older and closer to death you fool... yippee! (Although I do like giving and receiving prezzies so I go along with it obviously, what am I? Crazy?) I even made myself a sock puppet of Morrissey for my fortieth, well, no one else was going to.

1 YEAR CLOSER!

Wanted to

Wanted to join a crazy band, have parties, arty friends,
make lots of dosh and spend, spend, spend!
on silly things, purely aesthetic
a notion not at all pathetic

Wanted to travel far and wide
with a little pet monkey by my side
wanted to live a simple life with chickens at my feet
walk barefoot in clean fresh fields, bathed in summer heat

Wanted to make a new invention,
find a cure for cancer, my intention
then go flying in my jet to trendy places
and mingle with people with interesting faces

witty, talented, deep and real
with stacks of savvy and sex appeal
wanted to find my own true self, someone just like me
wanted to make a difference, wanted to be free

wanted to stay twenty-two, have confidence and charm
drive my converted Merc. along a deserted beach to my converted barn
Wanted to have long thick, shiny hair, matching lashes too,
big green eyes and perfect teeth which sparkled just like new

wanted to... still do.

Apps for everything...

All familiar with applications? App-arently you can get one for just about anything! If your pet budgie gets a peculiar rash on it's elbow, there's an app. for that. If your granny runs off with the window cleaner dressed as Lady Ga Ga, there's one for that too. But I'd like to know who's making all these apps. and will there ever be enough hours left in anyone's sad life to use them all? Do I care?

I have a dodgy old moby that wouldn't look out of place on the antiques road show, (neither would I come to think of it!) Which is perfect for my modest requirements. I never turn it on, keep losing it and I only text when I'm bored.

I don't know or wish to know how to use any of it's other magical witchcrafty, powers! (I do know it can only take atrocious photos and has no means of transferring them to anywhere!) What's the point of that? It's like a chocolate fire-guard, completely and utterly useless! (Although that's not the best example as that wouldn't be completely useless as you could scoff it then go and buy a proper one). But you get the drift.

Vampire, In Harrogate?

Now not only am I hyper sensitive to noise and smells but also I cannot abide bright lights! And after watching numerous horror films I am coming to the slightly disturbing conclusion I may be a vampire as I don't like confined spaces (especially coffins!) And I do like to wear mainly black and stay out late on a Friday night! My eyes also go very bloodshot too.

I don't like steak either! And I am very pale as I never sunbathe! I do love garlic though. It's a tricky one. No wait, I don't drink blood but then I do like to sleep in all day when I get the chance!...

It's official then, I am a closet vampire with issues... Must be an app. for that too!

Proper jobs...

Why do you never see proper jobs for proper people? You know, jobs you'd love to do for the best part of your life and of course a very respectable wage...

> **WANTED!**
> CHOC-MUNCHING SUGAR JUNKIE
> For immediate start.
>
> Experience preferred but full training available. Must have an addictive personality and finger licking ex perience. Self loathing, chubby chompers welcome. Overtime optional and free dentistry provided.

Talking of jobs I once saw an ad, in the classified section for a 'pig person' which instantly intrigued me, especially the person bit. Was it asking for someone with skills in piggery? If so, my lack of table manners are something to behold! I could be that "pig person!"... or was it a typo and they just wanted a BIG person?... Doh! Life's hard.

Follicle designers...

Hairdressers, are they becoming a cut above the rest? Elitist? Delusional more like! I ask because not only have I just staggered from a four hour hairdressing appointment eighty five quid lighter looking like Ken Dodd and Andrew LLoyd Webber's weird love child! I now have the hair of a baby oran utang! I even took in my photo of Angelina Jolie (to give them a challenge and a good chuckle!) but ended up more like her evil, bitter, twin sister "Anything-but Jolie".

They aren't even hairdressers anymore, no, they're "follicle designers" or "art directors!" They don't fool me... Why aren't they more honest? You never hear them ask "would you like to look ten years older? Like your mum perhaps or this month's latest hot look, one of the Pogues? It might not be exactly what you had in mind but at least we'd know what we were in for.

Proper jobs...

I'm not done yet...

What do you get after you've re-mortgaged the house to pay for your highlights?... "Hello, I'm Tracy your follicle fumbler for today... Can I take your coat?... Handbag?... Purse?.... Where do you live exactly?... Would you recognise me in a line up?...

Next the humiliating part where they hold up your hair as if it was radio active then ask "did you cut it yourself? No? Who did then? It's shocking! What a state!" You explain THEY did, 6 weeks ago, to be met with "Oh, doesn't it grow quick!"

"Right Stephanski, just wash her hair will you and try not to get soap in their eyes this time!" A bewildered Polish guy tentatively leads you to the sink, whereby the taps emit steam or ice and nothing in between. As your skull shrinks with the shock, you grasp the chair, already scarred from previous victims and close your eyes.

not yet but nearly...

The harsh rubbing of the towel on your head soon alerts you to phase three. Stephanski asks you to "Walk this way please" as he minces towards the "chair of doom". You answer in your mind (I would but I'd need surgery!)

You know things aren't going to plan when people start looking at you in sympathy with a "thank God it's not me" expression. (And that's just the stylists!)

"No, no need to show me the back thanks, I've got a good idea already (if the front's anything to go by!) No, I don't need hair spray, just get me out, now"... "How much?... Jesus H Corbett!"

You spend the next 3 months in hiding with an array of hats, mustering up the courage to be seen in public without terrifying babies! Or is it just me?

Holiday anyone?

They used to be things we aspired to, looked forward to and saved up ages for. The excitement of flying! The anticipation, counting off the weeks, days. Now it's just a complete drag, queues, delays, airport rip-offs, security gone mad. It's a relief to get home!

Soon they'll be paying us to go abroad coz we're wising up, fast! Do you really want to share the same air as that dodgy looking oik sat coughing up hairballs and scoffing cheesy wotsits? Or being forced to watch Star Trek Voyager again? Course not.

If you must travel, go by ship. Much more relaxing and you'll see more places, although typhoons, pirates and extortionate prices will eventually catch up with you. (Did I mention I worked for the tourist board?) Better to stay at home with some choccy biccies and watch "A place in the sun". Job done.

Swimming. Flapping around in other people's bodily fluids really isn't my idea of fun! If you've ever inhaled a verruca you'll know what I mean. You go in relatively healthy and come out looking like that tentacled octopus thingy from Pirates of the Caribbean. (Not a good look!)

The chemicals and bacteria alone could kill you (if that 20 stone kid jumping on your head doesn't get you first!)

For someone who doesn't even like touching door knobs, swimming in public pools is a bit of a worry. In fact it's a no brainer, unless you've got your own, you're asking for trouble. As for steam rooms.... don't get me started!

Watch the birdie!

My very first trip to Anglesey Wales was memorable for all the wrong reasons and has scarred me for life! Now I'm sure it's full of lovely friendly people and spectacular scenery but if I never go again it will be too soon.

My school friend had invited me to join her and her parents for a week in a rented cottage to this intriguing place I'd never heard of before. Even though I spent every summer in a caravan in Tenby! I was very excited at the idea of not having to spend it with my own family and relished the freedom! All that time to go off exploring! Couldn't wait!

Well the inevitable day finally arrived and we set off for another endless journey of traffic jams and bumpy roads but I kept my vision alive and pondered the possibilities. I awoke to the excited sounds of "we're nearly in Anglesey! Wake up! My heart thudding I looked out into a sea of rain and thought we'd landed on the moon. I'd never seen a place so flat! So... uninspiring, so...

Just as we drove through the main street along the front I spotted the sea. A forboding slate grey, but hey, it was the sea! Things will pick up soon I told myself, everything looks a little sadder in the rain (apart from Paris).

I spotted a sea gull, then another and soon the sky was full of these amazing creatures! Mesmerised by their majestic swoops I wondered what it must feel like to fly around with your mates all day. No rules, just living in the moment. We approached a short tunnel so I prepared to hold my breath (which I always did as a kid until we emerged) no matter how long they were. This time I held it for another reason completely. One which would scar my vision of this lovely place forever.

Beware!

Welcome to Anglesey!

As soon as we entered the noisy, bustling tunnel I watched a huge, hapless gull flap down and head straight for the bonnet. I froze then felt the sickening thuds under my feet which seemed to last ages. I visualized the true horror of what was happening beneath as it was introduced to the front bumper right along to the back. "Jesus H!" Cried her dad, "There goes another one!" As the car jolted and rattled with every breaking bone.

He didn't even slow down. Then her mum said "Must have been a fat bugger that one!" I was stunned for a moment then asked if it had happened before.

"Oh yes, daily around here, you just get used to it. Stupid birds, any one for a Polo?" My friend smiled at me nonchalantly and reached for a mint. I still felt sick and looked back to see flapping wings and scattered feathers hoping it was not suffering. Luckily it was just the howling wind, the gull was toast. It wouldn't have known a thing.

You guessed it, the rain continued to fall heavily all week and there was nothing to do. We didn't go swimming, didn't go anywhere around the cottage and worse still, no other kids around for miles. Felt like a State penitentiary that ruddy place and we didn't have any bikes either!

I was stuck! I've no recollection of anything else apart from how flat it was (not the gull, Anglesey) The place I witnessed my first murder and my first bee sting! (I also fell into a mass of nettles and no, doc leaves are utterly useless!)

I'd never been so relieved to return home. I thanked them for a "memorable" holiday and vowed never to go back, just in case it happened again.

Go take a hike!

There's no better place to be than up a mountain with lots of butties and a hot flask. When I lived in Lancashire we'd head for the Lakes with a spring in our step ready for a good old ramble. What we didn't expect was a severe case of the munchies! Bounding back down "The old man of Conniston" I began to notice I was getting faint with hunger (although we had devoured the contents of our ruck sacks just a couple of hours earlier.

This wouldn't be a problem for most normal people as they'd just wait till they got home but this was me and I was hungry. "You wouldn't like me when I'm hungry". I screamed "get me some food, nosh, anything NOW! Or I swear I'll have to find somebody!". Hubs looked terrified! "No, not to eat, to beg for food!" And we had to do just that. (Well, I had to).

Trembling and faint, I spotted a lone hiker oblivious to my plight. I must have been a little too exuberant as he looked scared as I tried to catch up with him, shuffling along loose rocks like a hunchback. My wayward rucksack, dishevelled hair and unsteady steps made him hasten his pace so I had to practically chase him which made things worse! Weak and shaky, I asked if he could spare a morsel of food, anything.

Relieved I was not about to mug him, he took pity on my predicament and assuming I was out with my carer, handed me some peanuts. I munched them like a savage and instantly felt the energy surge through my weakened frame. He chose this moment to escape so I never got the chance to thank him as he really saved my bacon that day.

Now I take emergency nibbles just popping to the shops.

Looks sheepish

Sheep are special, sheep are wise
sheep can fool us in disguise
they are not at all how they appear
sheep party hard throughout the year
they don't just wander aimlessly
sheep plot to conceal their identity
to lead a double life of fun
they're smart and savvy, far from dumb
even sneaking off to catch a movie
think they're cool, fab n' groovy
sheep even look you in the eye
and have the perfect alibi
climbing hills to pull daft faces
they all have friends in very high places
not at all meek and mild
sheep are reckless, crazy, wild!

Cripes! Which is worse?

Down under? Down right dangerous more like! I've always wanted to visit Australia but the more I think about it and the more I read... well you wouldn't would you?

(In a typical Aussie accent)...
"Cripes! You just poppin' out for a stroll in the 110 degree heat and choking humidity with yer iron lung and a bladdy great black mamba bites yer backside!

Dead in seconds. If you survive the mamba, a bladdy great pack of dingos track you down and rip your arms off! Cripes!... And if you survive the dingos, you might just make it to the beach, where a bladdy great white lurches at you from the surf and rips yer legs off!

If you survive long enough to make it back to shore, a bladdy great croc grabs you and wrestles you back into the water where, you guessed it, a bladdy great blue ringed octopus stings the hell out of your one remaining limb! If that doesn't kill you and you make it to the ambulance, think you're safe?

Think again! A bladdy great black widow lunges at you from under the blanket! Cripes!

(In a typical Northern accent)...
Better to stay here in good old rip-off, freezing Britain! The only deadliest, creepiest, most life-sucking, vile monster we have over here is the ruddy tax man! (Look, if I start mentioning the greedy bankers, the bent MP's etc. we'll be here all day).
Alledgedly.

I'm still planning to go to Australia, all that raw, stunning natural landscape and free heat, mmm... heat! Wow. It's got to be worth the risk as long as I go well prepared. (Hope I get past airport security in my e-bay space suit).

Feline facts

Aren't cats and kittens such cuddly, snuffly woofly, cute, adorable creatures? No! far from it! They're deceiving us! Toying with our pathetic human emotions!... Yes they offer companionship but so does "friends reunited" (and they don't poop in your shoes!)... Well there was that one occasion...

Cats just laze around all day, stay out all hours, leave hairs everywhere and have that nonchalant, cavalier attitude... "hey dude, keep the noise down OK? I'm trying to sleep here!" Cats, with their "holier than thou" attitude, who do they think they are? Yes I do have one but purely for recreational purposes (keeps me fit all that kicking!) Only joking, I think they have a psychic connection coz mine knows exactly what I'm thinking! Honest!

I only have to think about getting her some tuna and she's there, rubbing hairs all over my ankles so I go out looking like I've got moon boots on in the middle of summer!

I once had an amazing cat called "H". Not "H" from steps (coz, well that would be just disturbing!) no, "H' for Harrison.

He even had his own bachelor pad in the garden shed, kitted out with neon mood lighting, glitter ball, bar and superstar D.J "Fat cat slim! "He'd come staggering home at 4a.m, rat-arsed, stinking of alcho-pops and fish and wretching up hair balls then spend all next day in dark glasses sulking by the phone! Fond memories.

Cats have the upper paw!...

Who do they think they are? Sitting there with that face?
Just staring at you, motionless, same old place
waiting, watching, that knowing smirk
you try to ignore it but you can't (what a berk!)

They'll rub past yer ankles to grab your attention
or dig their claws in places you'd rather not mention!
covering your legs in fur and fluff
and if you complain they skulk off in a huff!

Five minutes later they're back in the house
with a special gift just for you, a half eaten mouse
Still it meows for food and treats
and wherever you go it gets under your feet

it's futile, hopeless you're such a wreck
those eyes, piercing right into the back of your neck
So you give in, you wish you had sooner
you grab the tin opener and reach for the tuna
yes I know it's a treat and it's only a cat
but she may go elsewhere and you wouldn't want that!

Joey to the rescue!...!

I love to rescue things, especially birds and recall grabbing the cat's jaws when I was about 7 and wrenching them open to allow a liitle sparrow to escape. Shocked, it just lay still so I shooed the cat away and prepared his new hospital bed. Birtrum was his name and although all the feathers were missing off his neck, no skin had been broken so I knew he'd have a good chance of surviving.

The good old cardboard box came out and I cushioned it with an old towel. He seemed fine and in just two days he'd eaten plenty of bread and milk (not the ideal diet here!) Then one day we heard a lot of tweeting from the windowsill and saw, I presumed, his mum coming to reclaim her missing son.

So I picked up the box and placed it outside, checking for cats first! What a lovely sight, his mum came and perched on the side to welcome him and what was the first thing she gave him? No, not a clip around the ear but some more bread which I'd thrown out earlier! His little face was a picture! (Just like when I give my kids vegetables!) They flew off together as nature intended and my job was done.

Don't look now...

One of my favourite pastimes is making people laugh when they really shouldn't. For instance, when my hubs is on the phone to his boss. When he works from home he's a sitting duck. I wait until he's deep in conversation about some important project and quickly stuff cushions down the front and back of my jeans and go outside the window where I know he'll be looking. I nonchalantly wobble past with a simple look on my face and maybe some bread sticking out of my teeth for comic effect.

I know this will completely destroy him and could possibly lose him his job but the thrill and fun of it just outweighs all the negatives! (Wonder if I still think that when we're living in a crisp packet on the M6).

Doggie do's and don'ts

Man's best friend? I don't think so... Not the huge monster I saw dangling from my neighbour's crutch! Savaged him big time. It was meant to be a guide dog! It must have gone berserk when the guy had his cataracts done and it realized it was out of a job! A labrador cross it was. (Cross alright! And so were his eyes! Ouch!) He didn't see that one coming.

I had a lovely border collie when I was a kid called Skipper (no I wasn't called Skipper, the dog was). I don't know why though coz he'd never seen a ruddy boat! But he was so clever and well mannered. He'd pick us up from junior school (no, not in a zooped up fiesta kind of way, wearing a fake Rolex! "Hey it's 3.30 dudes, hop in!") No, he'd just meet us at the school gate and escort us home. Rounding me and my sister up like sheep at exactly the same time without fail. (He even knew not to bother on weekends!) Brilliant dog! And I trusted him with my life. He was my protector, my companion and my first true love.

We lived on the moors in the middle of nowhere (in a house, obviously). So Skipper didn't need a poop a scoop as he had acres of green space all around. He just left his walnut whips anywhere he liked in the vast wilderness. The only complaints we got were from angry moles which had popped up at the wrong place at the wrong time looking like Ghandi exclaiming "pooh! Vot de bloody 'ellz dat?" Ah, I miss Skipper!

Something evil's lurking...

Now I walk everywhere these days. Even that's not safe! The amount of doggie do on the pavements is atrocious! There's so much of it around our way the traffic treats them like roundabouts, it's mayhem! And you'd think everyone has gone Michael Jackson crazy doing the "moon walk" everywhere but they're just trying to get the damn stuff off their shoes!

(To the tune of... Thriller: "something evil's lurking in the dark...").

Grandad's a "Hoodie"!

There he was, swearing like a trooper
with his fat bull terrier n' no pooper-scooper
looking "real 'ard" with his canine buddy
up to no good no doubt (coz he's wearing a hoodie!)

Can't see his face, all hidden n' slouched
What's he up to all shifty n' crouched?
Oh no, he's reaching for somethin' sharp, oh 'eck!
I'd best leg it fast or he'll stab me in t'neck!

Wait a sec, I know that grin...
those beady eyes n' pointy chin
it's Grandad! Grandad you silly o'wd sod!
you scared me rotten I swear to God!

What you playin' at? lurkin' round 'ere of all places?
you be at 'ome with yer feet up watchin t'races
"Ey up I've been walkin' neighbour's dog Buster
he's a rum 'un and I need all t'strength I can muster!

He pulls on t'lead n' poops like an 'orse!
it's three below zero n' t' winds are gale force!
I've run out of bags n' me hands are so stiff
but If don't keep on walkin' I might catch a whiff!

Me pocket's are burstin', no wonder I swear!
'Ere do us a favour take him 'ome, if you dare!
He's fat n' he's slow with no teeth and a limp
& Buster's no better, he's such a wimp

Don't know what he's been eatin' but it must 'ave some clout
coz all t' drivers think it's a roundabout!
I've diverted traffic three times already
Enough's enough, I'm off for a pint with Eddie!...

Budgies have rights too...

We love budgies so much we stuff them in a tiny cage so we can well, stare at them. And what if little Joey get's sad and lonely? Well we get him a mirror of course! And if he gets really depressed? A bell! Brilliant! So now he's living his whole sad little life like the Truman show! Being watched, no real friends, just talking to himself in a false reality! Falling in love with his own reflection... Blimey, sounds a bit too familiar! Moving swiftly on...

Talking of birdies, Pigeons! There are lots of theories about these amazing creatures... you know the one's which always have a gammy, stumpy foot. Well I have a theory too. It's not coz they're lame, it's because of all the chewing gum thrown onto the pavements in busy town centres. That's not their real foot, it's a huge clump of Wrigley's spearmint (or peppermint)! And their foot's inside perfectly fine just entombed in this sticky menace.

So next time you spit your gum out without a care, just have a thought for the poor pigeon that unwittingly picks it up on it's foot, and has to spend the next five years limping around collecting more and more until eventually it becomes a giant ball like in "The prisoner"... People having to run down the street screaming to avoid it like raiders of the lost Ark. Do you really want that on your conscience?

And while we're on the subject of conscience, stop nicking pigeon's jobs all you post men and women! Highly respected carrier pigeons were in full employment sixty years ago, raking it in and now where are they? Out on the streets, that's where, having to busk in shopping malls and dodge all the gum, just to earn an honest crumb. Shame on you!

Pets and people

I love animals but I have to question why we really keep pets and even the motives. I know they can be good company.. "oh my Freddy, he's such a love, there every day to greet me and he loves to watch countdown". Well he's no choice has he? If he did, what would he choose? A. Sit at home all day watching TV or B. complete freedom? Mmm, it's a toughie.

Let's be honest, we keep pets for our own selfish enjoyment. (Myself included). We can't own anything really so we're just fooling ourselves! It's quite immoral. We can rescue them, nurse them back to health but we should never deny them freedom to roam their planet. It's so last year, just like fake tan.

I know it's an unpopular idea... but in years to come keeping "pets" will be frowned upon in horror (like smoking or Simon Cowell's trousers!)

Be treated like a dog...

I wouldn't have believed it if I hadn't seen it with my own eyes but people actually PAY other people to shout at them (and in a rather condescending manner!) The occasion? Boot camp style fitness classes and personal trainers!

Paying someone to shout orders at you. World's gone mad! If you get your kicks being humiliated and treated like a dog then fair enough but pay? There's a much simpler method and it's absolutely free...

I'll come round any time and scream at you and you won't even have to dress in unflattering spandex and look like a complete numpty (unless of course you particularly like that sort of thing).

"Oy YOU! yes YOU! Get your gargantuan backside off that couch NOW! You worthless piece of lard!... Fifty sit-ups now! Simple. Any time you like. I won't charge you a penny. Just a cuppa will do, no sugar thanks and go easy on the semi-skimmed.

A typical date in the fairytale land of Romance.

You take seven hours getting buffed, plucked and de-fuzzed, smelling like a living advert for body shop. You spend over an hour choosing "the right outfit", handbag, accessories, perfume, shoes. The anticipation is electric! Then reality kicks you up the jacksy! "He's late! The cheeky get is bloody well late!" Just then he phones to explain his Reliant Robin isn't well, reliant at all.

In fact he's stuck on the M6 scrounging a lift off a cross dressing trucker who goes by the name of Garyanna! Finally turns up two hours later reeking of oil and sweat (and not in a good away!) Clutching a Maccy D! "Thought we'd eat in coz it's getting late"... Whoopee!

Does this ring any bells? Have you known a bloke like this? First few dates he starts off so polite and gentlemanly, even opening your car door... "oh allow me" and suggesting exciting venues for the next date and within a matter of weeks he's not only forgotten how to open doors, but seems to have mysteriously undergone a frontal lobotomy coz his whole character has changed!

Now he's belching, farting, picking bits out of his nose, ears, belly button... and fiddling with his crotch while watching tellly. I'm sure he didn't do that before...?

Then all those exciting nights out have mysteriously turned into comfy, predictable nights in, falling asleep on the sofa then waking up with a sweet n' sour chicken ball stuck to your eyelid. Or is it just me?

And are'nt tight, mean swines so unattractive? Male or female, if you're stingy, stay home ok? It's not a good look. You know who you are.

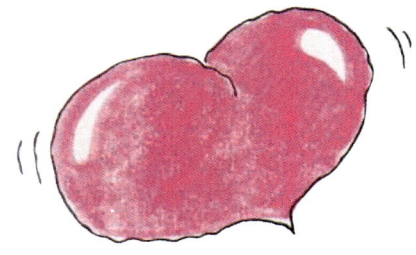

A (hopefully not so typical) proposal.

Romance. Just save yourselves! It's just nature's way of lulling you into a false sense of security! My life's not really been much like "Officer and a gentleman", more like "half-wit and a bigot". Most women dream of a fairy-tale proposal and many are lucky enough to get it! Not me, no... mine was a little more... what would you say "nightmare proposal from hell?" Yes I remember it well and I don't let him forget it either! It was the biggest let down since MC Hammer found religion!

Let's see if you can beat this one. We'd gone camping (not that "chase me with a feather duster" kind of camping but the real "billabong, ging gang goolie goolie gotcha" kind with mouldy tent, damp sheets and creepy crawlies! Real camping, in a tiny village called Dent. We'd been to the only pub (well there was nothing else!) And He got well and truly rat-arsed on whisky and beer while I got tiddly on just half a shandy. We staggered back to our tent, steaming... from the rain and just as I was about to doze off, he mumbled "shall we get wed?" This caught my attention coz I wasn't expecting that... or anything else for that matter! But before I could answer he just ran outside half naked to honk up all over the field, it was like trying to avoid land mines on his way back to the tent from hell and he emerged reeking of vomit with an assortment of mixed veg stuck to his teeth (and toes).

"Was it the drink or the idea of marrying me that pushed him over the edge?" I wondered. Next morning came these rather special words... "yes, course I remember asking and I was serious, just don't go telling everyone ok? And don't expect an engagement do either, you know I hate parties".

Ah, romance... (Good job he makes up for it in lots of other ways!)

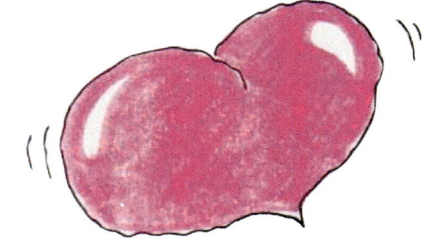

Likes and loathes.

New Romances
Second chances
Nice hot cuppa tea
Bargain bucket just for me
Lazy TV dinners
Guilt free sinners
Squeeezing soft, warm putty
Cheese and jam butty
Picnic treat
nice warm feet
Twiddling my hair
Soft, new underwear
Stroking the cat
My turn to bat
A sherbet dabble
Winning at Scrabble
Roast spuds and gravy
Hair straight, not wavy
The scent of sweet peas
Finding your keys
Blueberry pie
That look in your eye

Screaming kids
Unscrewable lids
Wind and hail
Direct mail
Appalling manners
Baddly spelllt bannerrs
Shameless braggers
Free speech gaggers
Stingy drizzlers
Turkey twizzlers
DVD's on fitness
Jehovas witness
Endless queues
Dog shit shoes
Whopping bills
Dentist drills
Hairy arm pits
Two faced gits
TV repeats
Lying cheats
People who shout
Bums hanging out

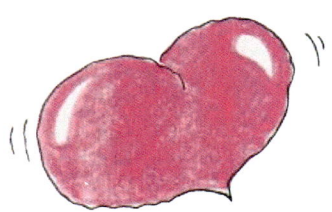

Should've known...

Whilst posing at the bar, eyeing up this lovely fella,
I got stabbed in the eye with my cocktail umbrella!
Well I hid the pain, as best as I could
but my make-up went AWOL down my cheek, well it would

There, you guessed it, now he's looking right over
thinks I'm a drunk but I'm stone cold sober
To think I paid all that for a bit of crushed ice
I'm a cheap-skate and bitter, it doesn't look nice

It's just such an effort, trying to impress
when you're uncomfy in anything which resembles a dress
he probably thinks I'm a bloke in drag
Well I'm feeling quite butch and I look like a hag

Oh it's not really me, I shouldn't really be here
I'm feel such a berk and a little bit queer
such a waste of money, such a waste of my time
why didn't I stay in and just gone on-line?

Stereotypes, you wot?

Isn't it weird we make our minds up about people in seconds based on their accent! We can't help it can we? Apparently the most trusted accent in the U.K. is Geordie - Newcastle. Why eye man! So the telemarketing companies like to use them for cold calling... "Could a talk to the home owner please? Eye, Sorry luv? Ya cannae tell what am talkin' aboot? Well a cannae help that! We cannae all come from Newcastle ya knowz"... Trust nobody.

And the Oyrish. Why do we like to think they're all thick? No idea. My cousin was Oyrish so he was! He taught bank holidays were just for Bankers! "Well that's alroyt for those lucky sods" He said "but what about the rest of us? (Ok I made that up). I'm half Irish so don't be offended.

And the Welsh! Oh yes, the wonderful singing Welsh. With their tall funny hats and strange language! Tom Jones! Now that's a good welsh name isn't it boyo? And boy can he sing! Shame about the language though, all that Gogogoch n' clan fer fechn! Must be all that damp weather and slate. You never know if they're speaking or just clearing their throat!

And of course the lovable lads n' lasses from Liverpool! Ah the cheeky, witty Scousers! People just don't trust them for some strange reason...

"Yeah, course you can park yer moter der mate! Nah, course it won't get nicked, I'll keep me eye on it for yeh n' watch out for the scallies! Sorted!... Safe as houses mate!... Ey Micky, get over 'ere sharpish n' bring yeh screw driver! It's Christmas!"

CITY ART INSTALLATION

More sterotypes...

And the Scottish! Oh the proud Scots! You cannae take the mickey out of those! With their auburn hair and tartan skirts! Eye, n' that's just the blokes! You know why they do all that highland dancing- you'd dance like that too if you were freezing your nuts off in just a skirt with no kecks on! Shame about the weather!

I once went to a loch in Scotland on one of the hottest days ever and decided to cool off with a paddle, so looking like the famous postcard from Skegness I ran in up to my knees and froze stiff! Shooting pains shot right up my legs and I had to be lifted out screaming in agony! Never, ever step foot in a loch! It's not "bracing" it's down right dangerous!

And not forgetting the Asians! Oh the Asians, they tank you a million times, so cheeky, so spicy, so very very nicey... so colourful the sari, so very dal a lami! so Punjabi, Abudabi... Ok.

Oh ze French! J'adore their passion, their beautiful, funny language and their arrogance! And what a beautiful place! So what, if we think they are all garlic munching egotists, I am too! And a teeny weeny bit arrogant so we have lots in common. I don't drink wine however but only because it gives me migraines and tastes like battery acid! (I expect a lot for £2.99).

France has a better climate too, loads more space and the history! Stunning! I'd love to retire there one fine day (or rainy day for that matter!)

The world would be such a boring place without stereotypes! Long live political incorrectness! Hurrah for free thinking and free speech!

"Bonjour"

Kinell Blue...

My first car was a tatty old Vauxhall and was my pride and joy. I'd saved up long hard for it although it was an odd colour but I didn't mind. Whenever I went anywhere people always enquired as to what colour it was exactly. (Yes, a boring question) especially time after time so I came up with the name "kinell" blue (as it was rather apt.) As they'd say "***kinell, what colour's that?" (They were never sure if it was an actual paint colour or a weird chemical reaction but I liked to keep people guessing). Well they shouldn't be so rude.

My first driving lesson was a complete fiasco too. My instructor was such an ancient, frail man who really shouldn't have been driving at all. He turned up in this tiny car which took him fifteen minutes just to get out of the damn seat! And when I did finally get behind the wheel he'd make me remove my shoe! (No he didn't have a toe fetish, well I don't think so.) I was just very heavy footed like "Pansy Potter" The strong man's daughter.

So I had to drive bare foot until I was much more gentle with the pedals. (Not too traumatic) you may be thinking but it has left me with a rather strange affliction. I like to drive without trousers and find it highly amusing to stop at traffic lights with a (fake) foot sticking out of the window.

And in an American left hand drive automatic car I used to have, I'd rest my right foot on the dash whilst driving! (Don't try this folks!)

So you can see this simple exercise has had a powerful (and slightly disturbing) effect on my delicate psyche.

You couldn't make it up

Why is it, a simple task like parking the car turns into a complete fiasco? It's a nice day, fairly quiet in town. You spot a parking space, bit tight but you're feeling lucky. Reversing slowly you spot two old dears who have just settled down on the wall near by to watch... you! "Hey hurry up Mildred, that's it, put your shopping down here. She's gonna try and park! Get t' flask out, it's gonna be good! Could be nasty, on a bit of a hill too, she'll never make it, miles off t' kerb. I daren't look" "Oh Doris, it's bad news, very bad..." "What? Oh no, don't say she's done it!" "F'raid so, better luck next time...".

Almost drowning in your own sweat after squeezing into a space which defies the laws of physics, you realize it's a ten minute zone! TEN minutes? That's not even enough time to get your seat belt off or grab your fake disabled sticker from the glove compartment! No wonder the council's making enough money to replace acres of bedding plants that would rival Elton John's extravagance! (You'd think they'd never heard of hardy annuals!)

You finally find a place to pay for this affront, a machine, that states "NO CHANGE GIVEN" How dare it keep my change? It's mine, not yours! Where else would we accept that without a second thought? You buy a loaf of bread and pay with a tenner and the assistant states "NO CHANGE GIVEN". Then continues to explain how your extra £8.86 will go towards the end of year rave and her tattoo habit.

Would you stand for it? Of course not so how do they get away with daylight robbery? Parking meters are just twenty first century Dick Turpins! (Now where did I park the damn thing?). Might as well sell it and buy a horse and a mask. I look good in black.

Ey, wot's 'appnin?

Modern art galleries! Youv'e all been there... trying to look like you visit them regularly and are interested in all things arty. Admiring the installations, stepping closer, stepping back, contemplating... a crowd forms around you as you study the hidden meanings and try and figure out just what the artist was trying to convey. You suddenly realize you're still in the foyer and the cleaner comes to pick up her bucket. Sooo embarassing yah?

Conceptual art: The "art" being the "idea behind it" ...yeah right. A light being switched on then off then on then... a row of bricks... a mop and bucket, or is it? I'd love to hang an enormous pair of gonads up and let everyone express what it really means... say what you see!

What is happening to our beautiful old English language? I'm all for harnessing various influences but we're all merging into Ali G! INNIT?

Even I'm starting to catch this unstoppable epidemic! And if you've no idea what I'm on about as you weren't born a million years BC (Before Coronation Street) then just listen to the amount of people who talk in text language... "Dat u fink is 'avin a LOL"

Is it just me? Am I becoming a grumpy old get? Statements are statements, questions are questions and correct spelling and pronunciation is important. Oh and by the way, it's YOU not CHOO... that's a sneeze.

When I'z talks like dis to me kids a just get 'owls o' laffin' man innit? O'w comes it's not cool when I'z does it? Is it just me likes or izzit anyone over forty? Take da shame.

Wot you starein' at?

Wot you starein' at man?
can't you seez who I am?
I'm a cool dude wiv me big designer shades
flashin' all me bling n' eyein' all de babes

I got da moves, I got it goin' on, hell I got da whole shebang
wiv me bad-ass bro's in me bad-ass gang
don't give me no grief wiv ya TK-Max bandanna
take the shame coz I'z flashin' Dolce & Gabana

you still starein at me'? You'd better get back-up
you're out numbered man, your odds, they don't stack up
Oh hello dad, er, really sorry about all that,
yes I know I'm a jerk and an annoying little... tw *t!

You just know you're in a rut when...

You whistle the whole theme tune to antiques roadshow... without laughing!

You sing along to "Go compare!" instead of flicking to another channel immediately.

You read all the Sunday supplement's adverts for "world's comfiest trousers" or "A slipper for both feet!" or "This year's must have slouch blanket" all the way through, fascinated and somehow compelled to purchase!

Your cat goes out more than you do, has more money and more friends.

You've had no texts for 3 weeks and even your "low battery indicator" can't be arsed to inform you!

You cry yourself... awake!

You no longer fancy George Clooney or Angelina Jolie and prefer to spend time with your pet stick insect Brian.

You just know you're getting on a bit when…

Eating cake becomes more important than basic hygiene!

You're either freezing cold or boiling hot & nothing in between!

You prefer to stay in with your stuffed dead dog Lucky and a cheap cooking sherry.

Out shopping for biscuits you spot a "scruffy-arsed troll" in a shop window then suddenly realize it's your reflection.

You start picking up other peoples' rubbish in the street, only to dislocate your hip!

You pop into clothes shops just to keep warm and to eat your home made butties.

All your mates look "ancient!"

You find tartan personal shopping trolleys strangely alluring, along with baggy, tan coloured pop socks and comfy slippers.

You have a secret stash of Worther's originals.

WHY IS IT?

Why is it every rotten time I try to do my best

something happens to foul it up and put me to the test?

For instance, when I'm in a rush and need everything at hand,

my gear will simply disappear on cue, to some far off, distant land

Or when I'm as skint as a poor church mouse

who's been wheel clamped once too often,

I'll see loads of stuff I'd love to buy - bargains galore and more

and then, you guessed it, when I'm flush (a rarity indeed!)

nothing catches my eye... except some airborne grit maybe and a rather painful fly.

All part of the bigger picture

When you bare your soul, raw and cold,
when you trudge through sludge laden down,
when you spend your precious time
and the future soon becomes the past,
when all your aspirations fade to indignation
you pause, then realise, you are a drop in the ocean,
a particle of infinity, insignificant yet so vital
you smile and wallow in the magic of consciousness.

Fear not, this isn't goodbye, it's "see you soon" for our next adventure! Take care and don't take life too seriously or it will be a short one! Take time to daydream and relish the simple things such as warm socks and Jaffa cakes. (But not warm Jaffa cakes, obviously).

Make lots of friends but not too many that they all blur into one great mass of acquaintances. And don't forget to keep well away from all things boring.

Thanks to all the kind people who unwittingly contributed to this book, including my family, friends and some complete strangers who just happened to be in the wrong place at the wrong time.

I hope it inspires you to write your own to pass down to your future generations. (Much better than a hideous ornament which ends up being bought for 20p at a car boot sale by a cross dressing pig person from Croydon).

QUESTION EVERYTHING

The basic philosophy of Joey Parkin. Artist.

www.joeyparkinartist.co.uk

 Why?

ALCOHOL-FREE FUN IN A BOOK!

G&T? is a tasty tonic, to be absorbed daily for maximum effect. It contains lots of funny and often poignant snippets, observations, poems and sketches to give you "the feel-good factor".

This will last far longer than any other stimulant (without the nasty side effects).

"I strongly recommend you purchase this book, now!"
Joey's accountant

"It' sucks!"
A pig farmer from Croydon

Printed in Great Britain
by Amazon.co.uk, Ltd.,
Marston Gate.